I0419879

NAME that ANIMAL
Christmas Coloring Book

A simple, easy way for kids to learn the names of animals. And coloring pages for them to color them. Love the coloring of your artist? Frame It! Watching your child's excitement will make your Christmas!

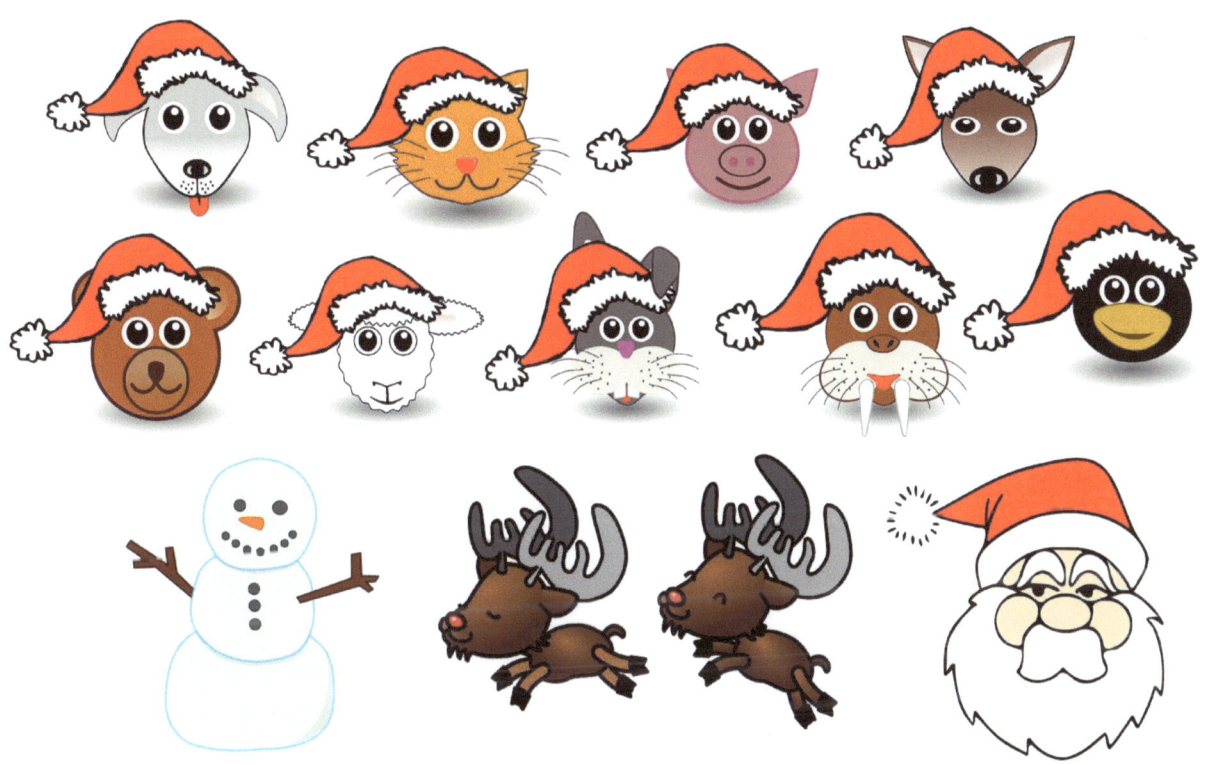

I Am A

_ _ _

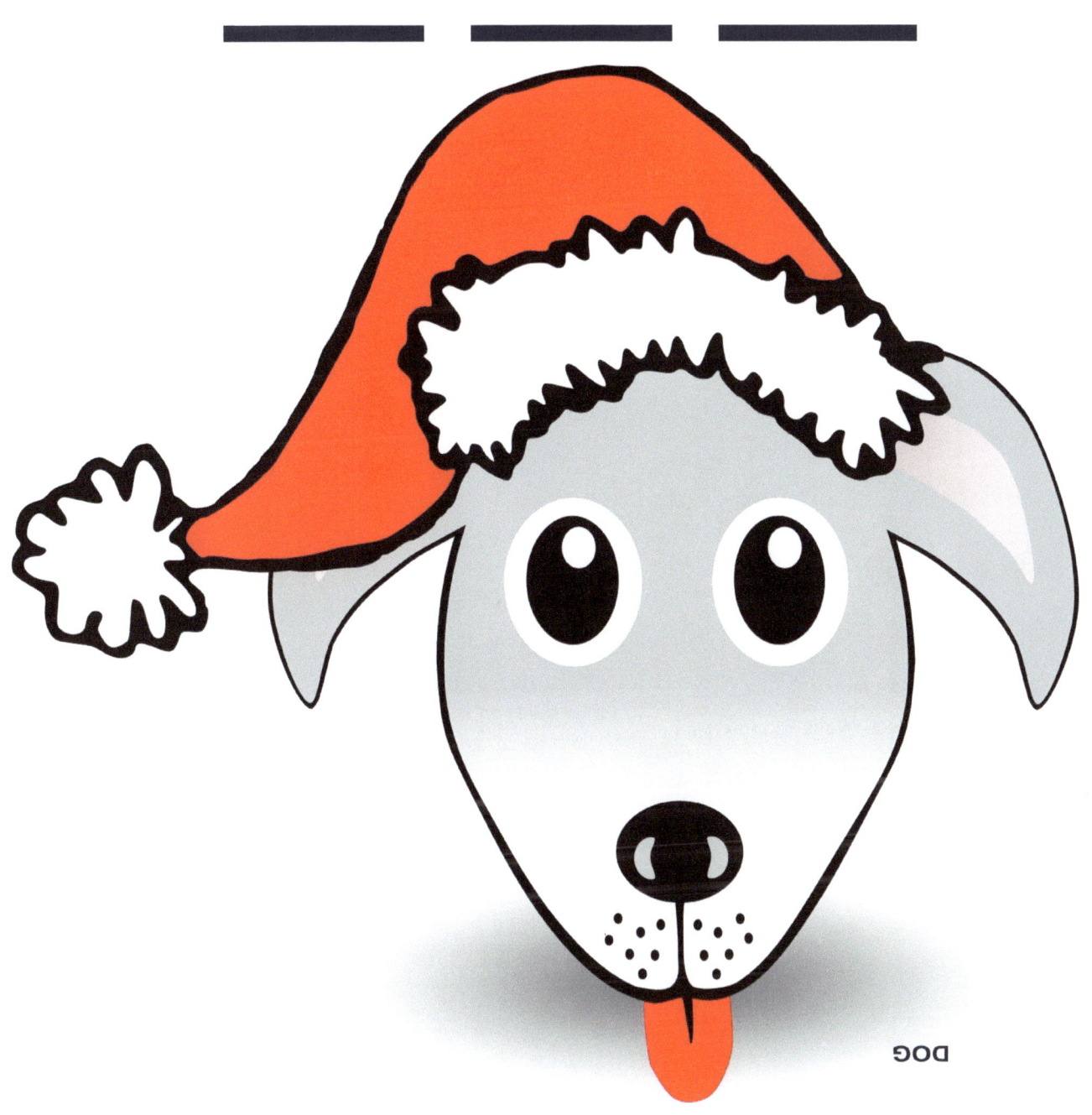

DOG

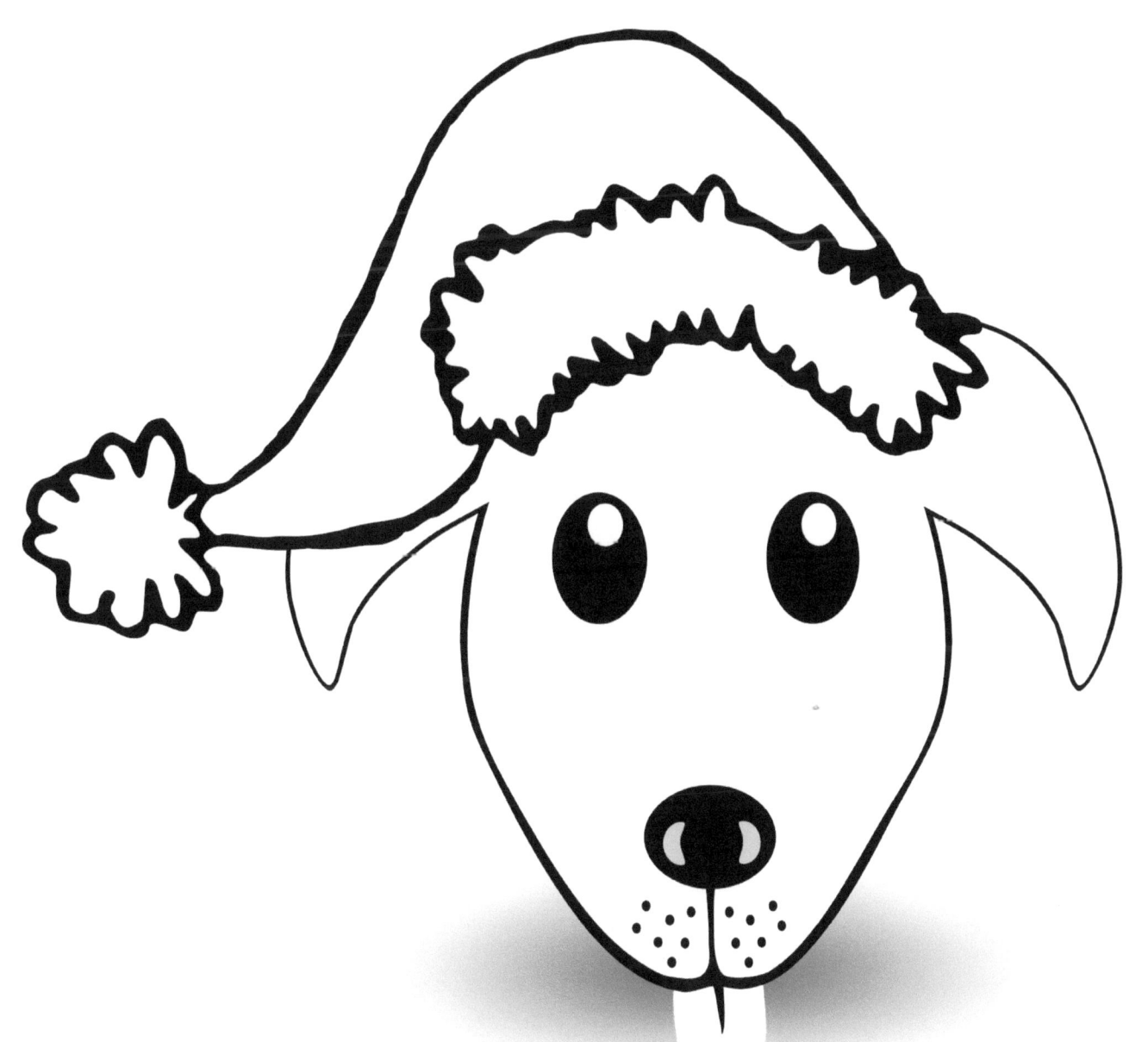

I Am A
D O G

I Am A

___ ___ ___

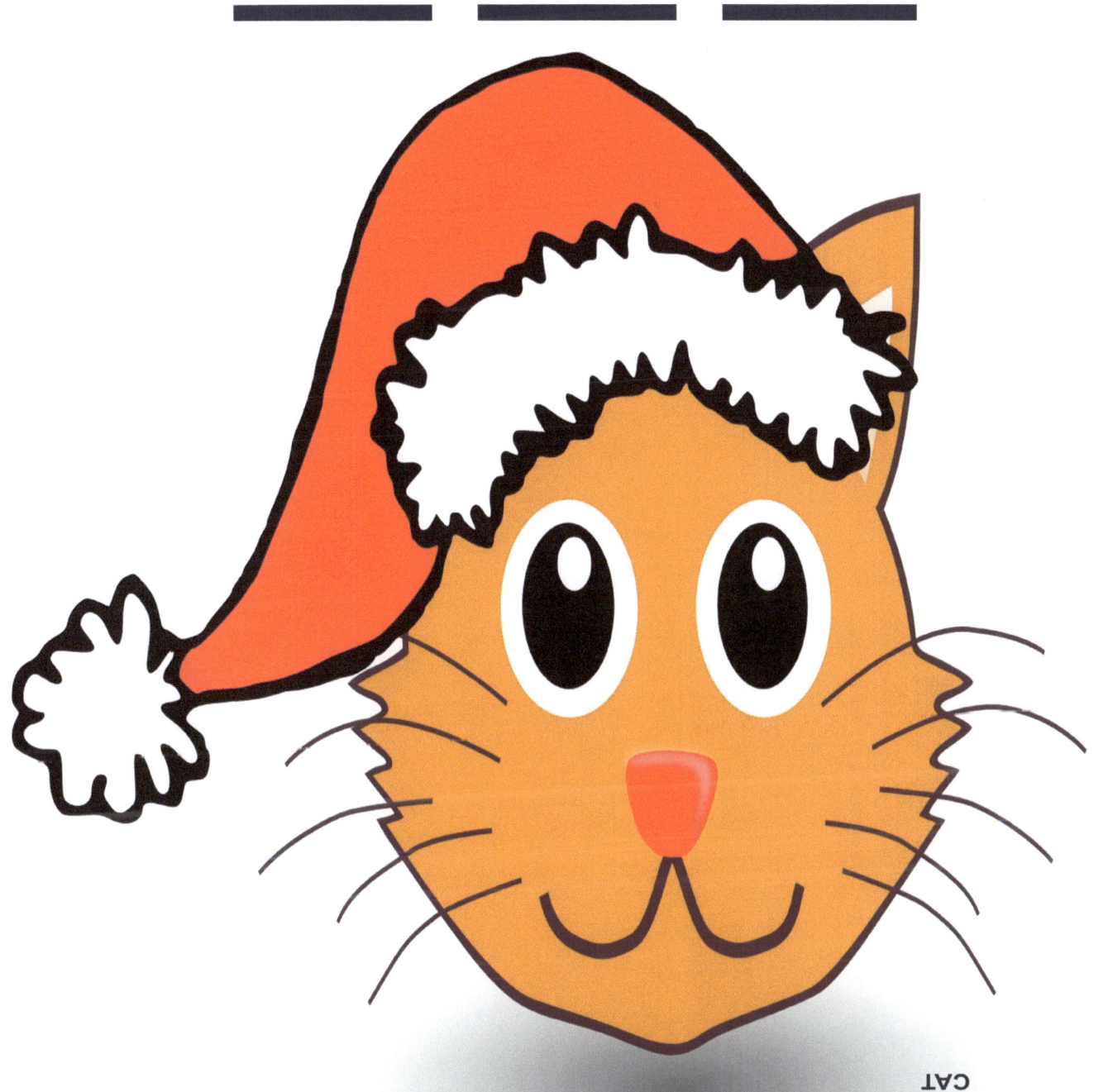

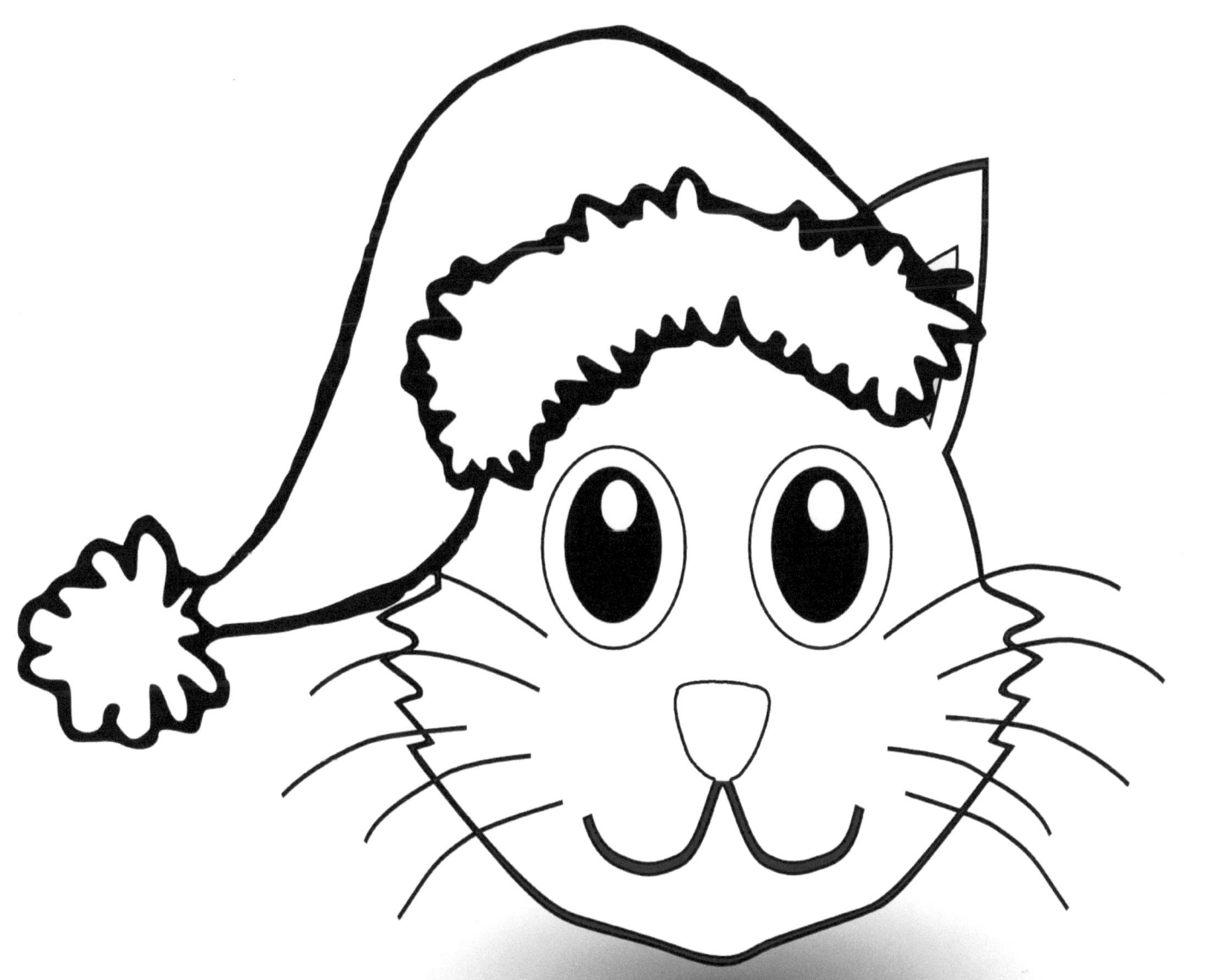

I Am A
C A T

I Am A _ _ _

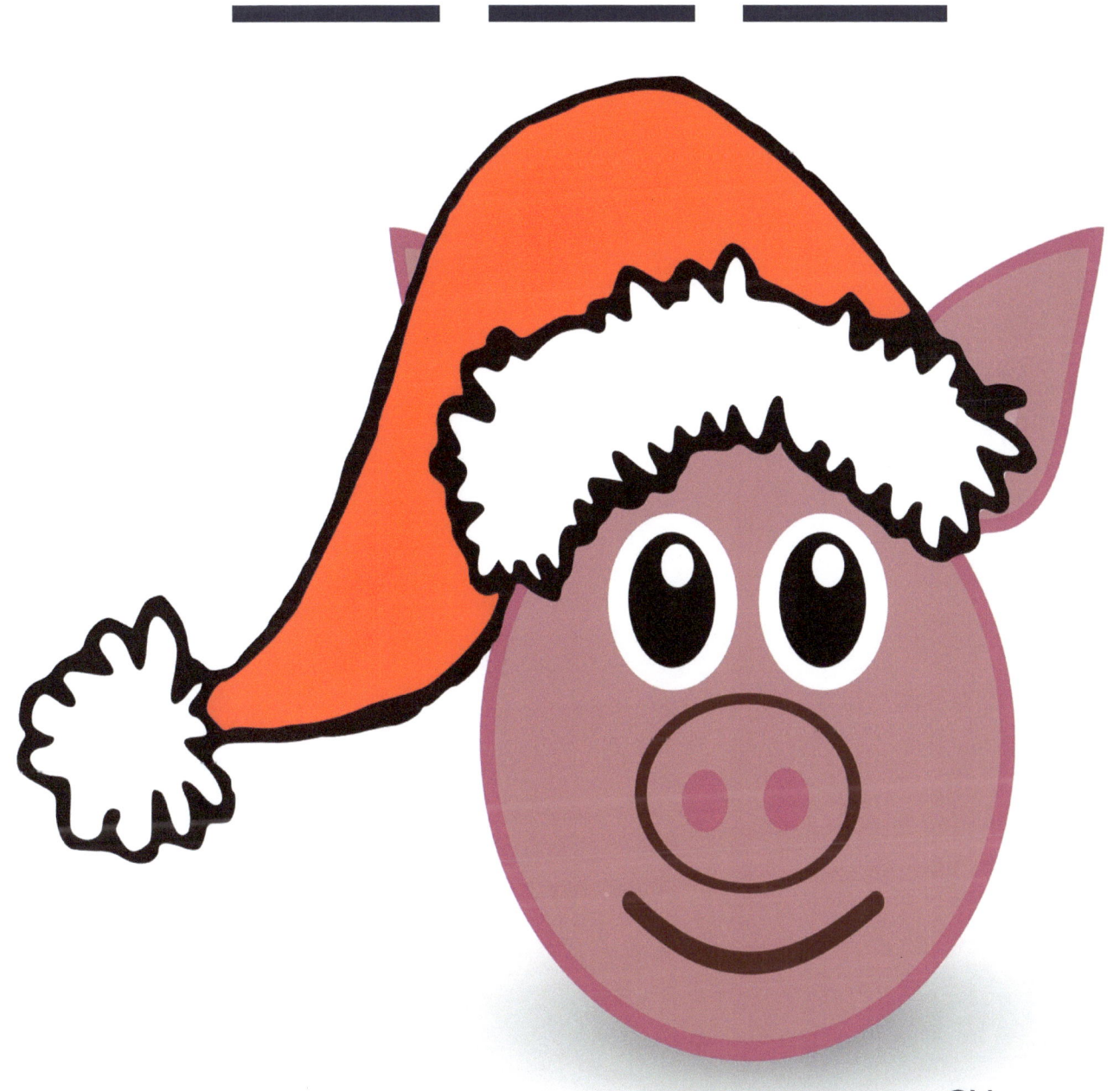

PIG

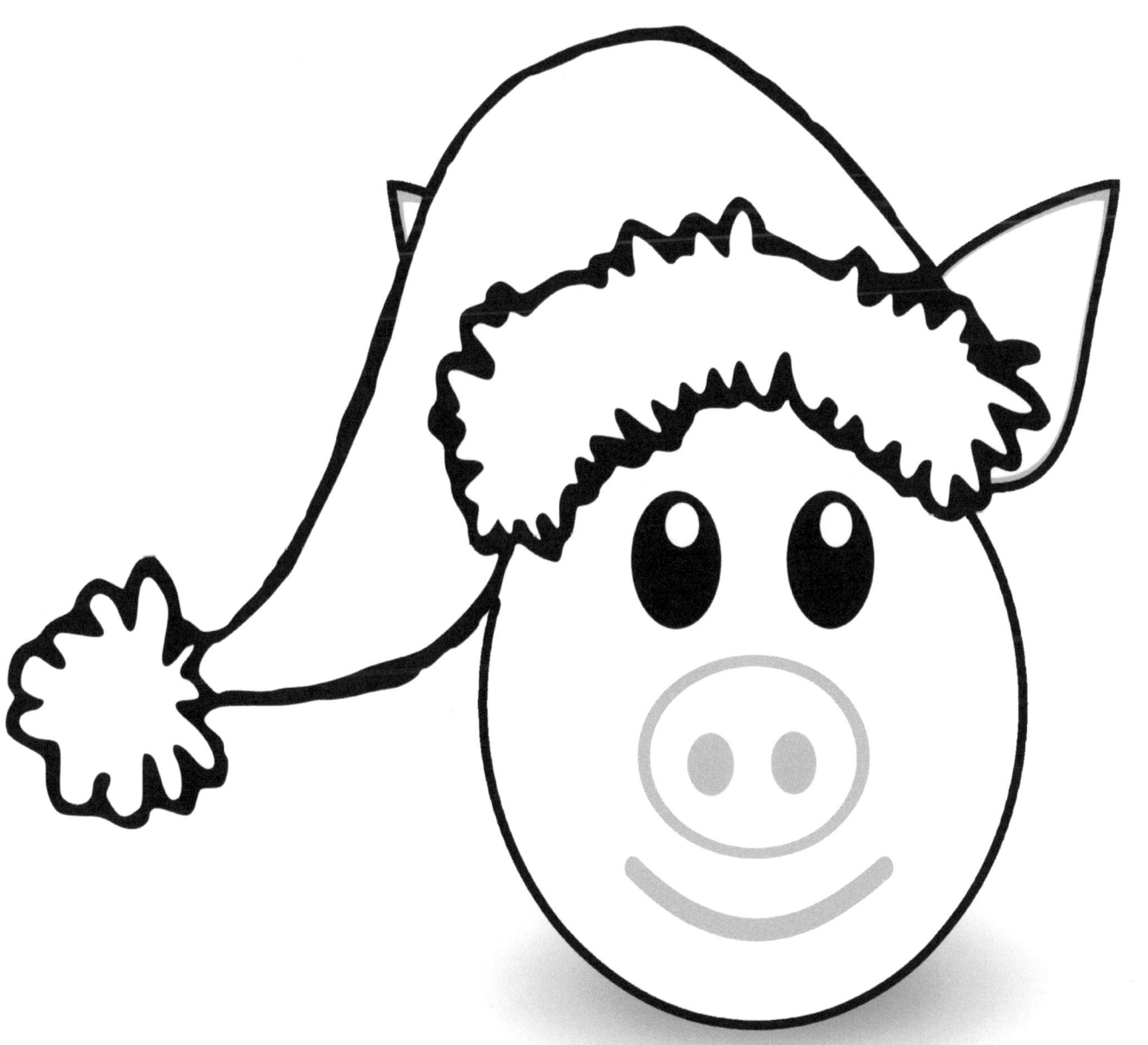

I Am A
P I G

I Am A

_ _ _ _

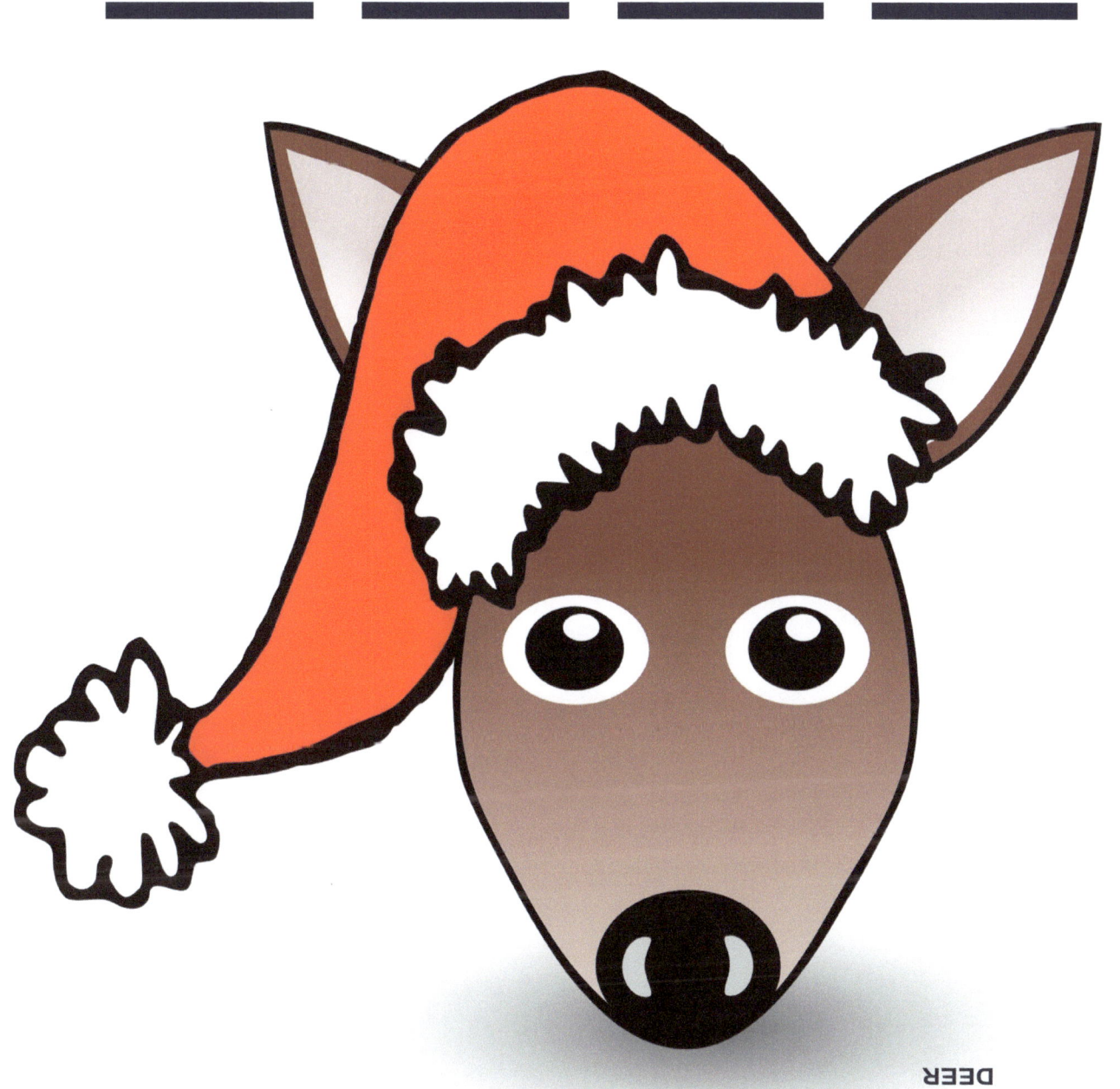

DEER

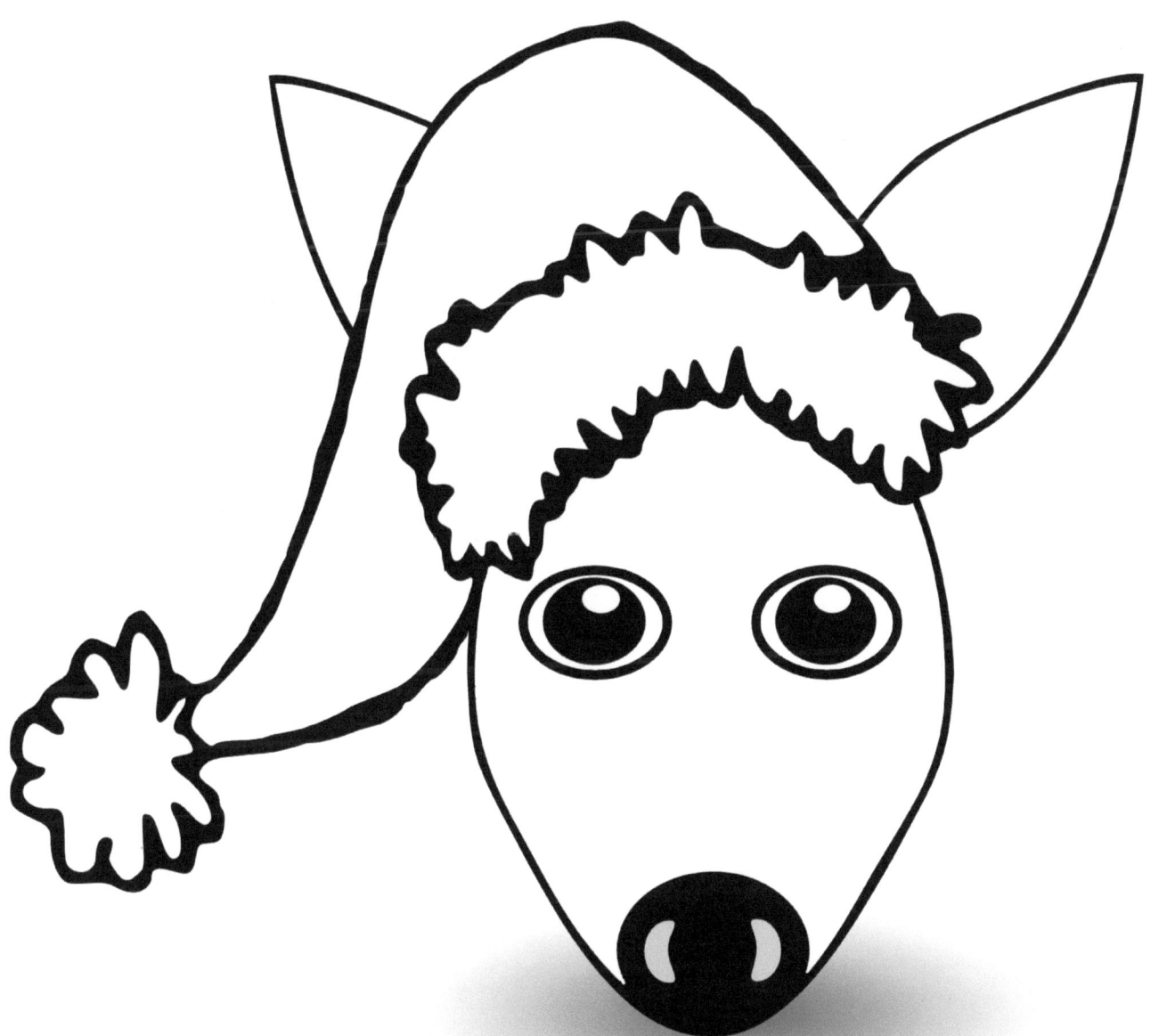

I Am A
D E E R

I Am A

_ _ _ _

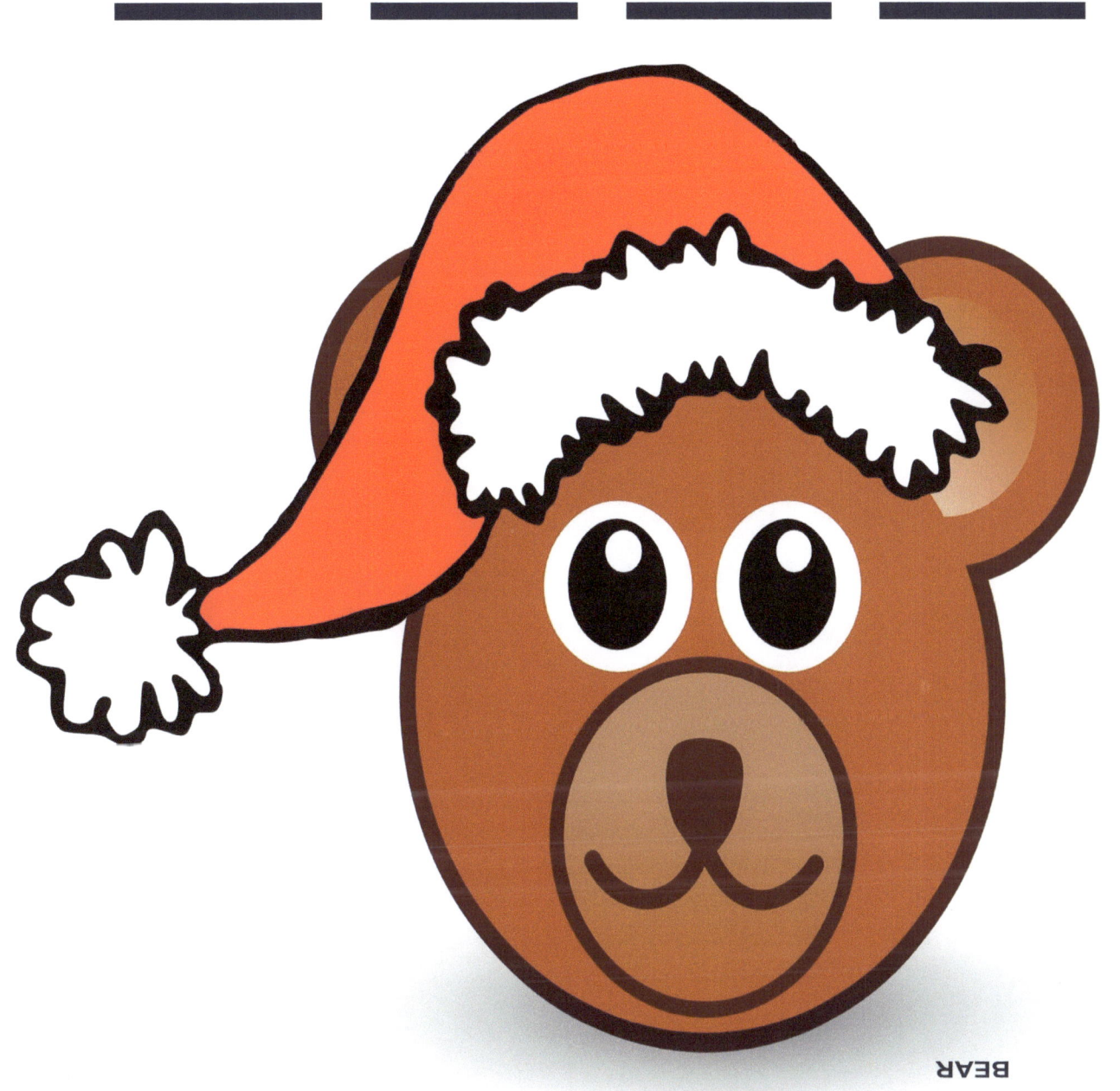

BEAR

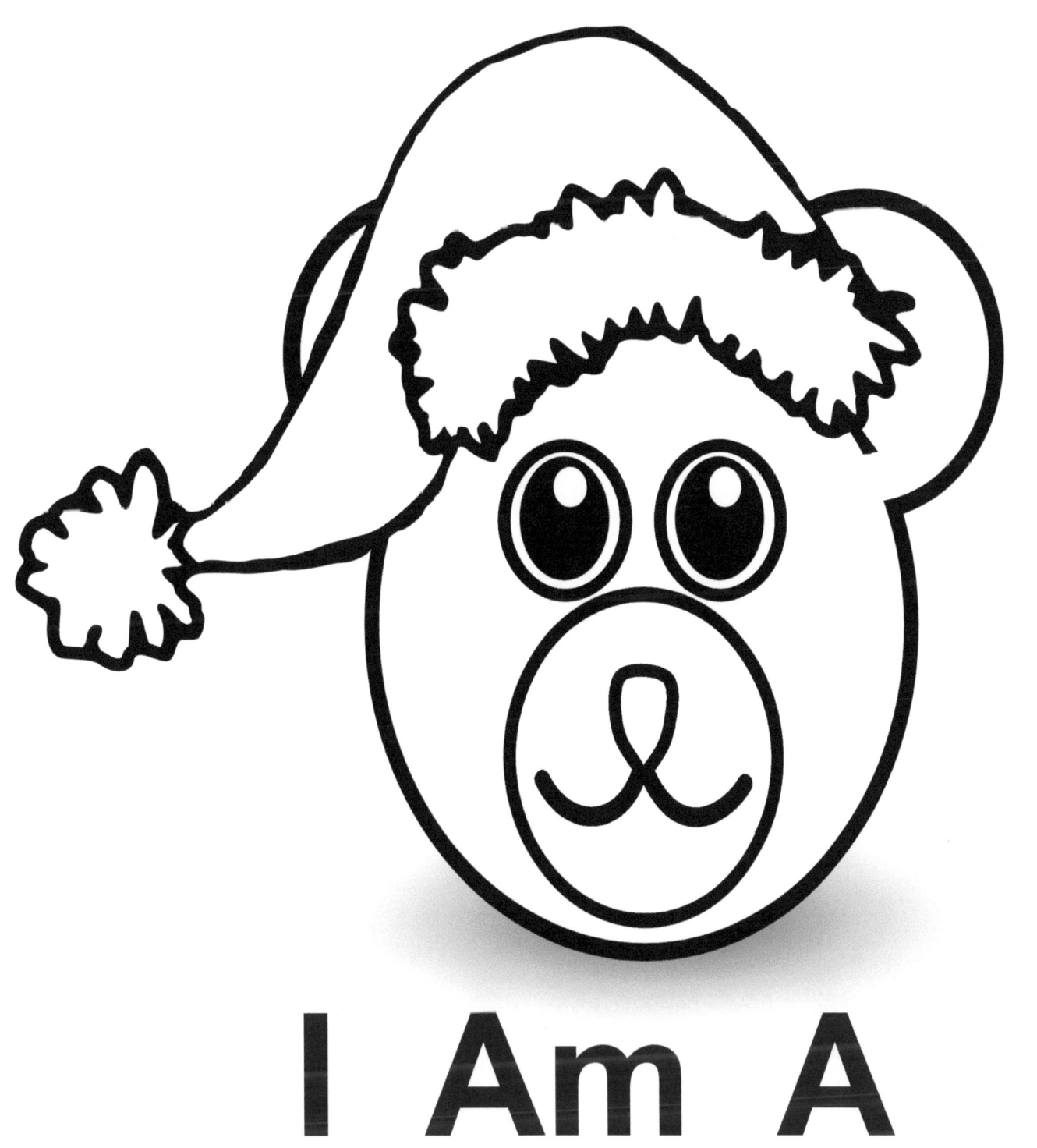

I Am A
BEAR

I Am A

_ _ _ _ _

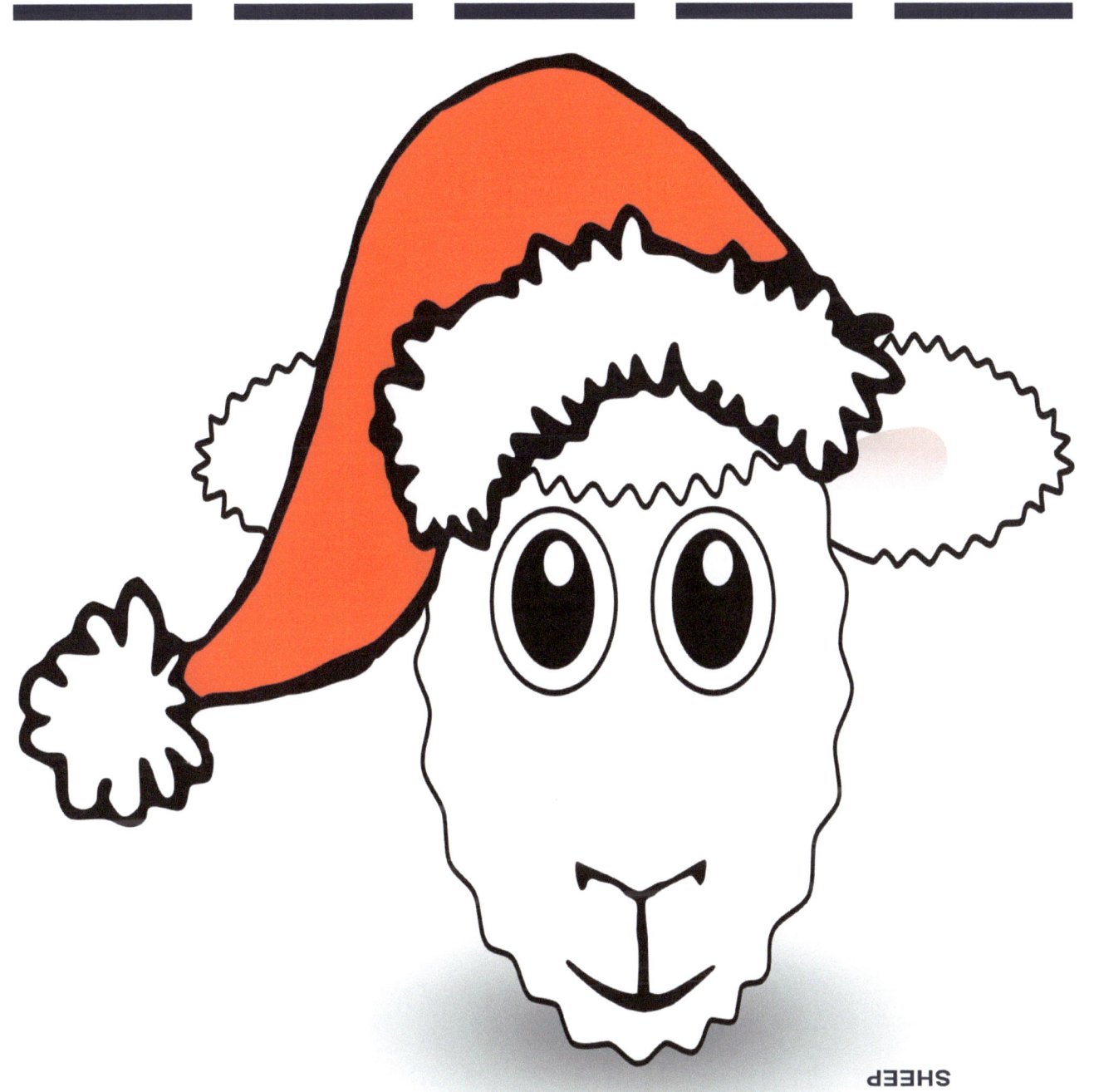

SHEEP

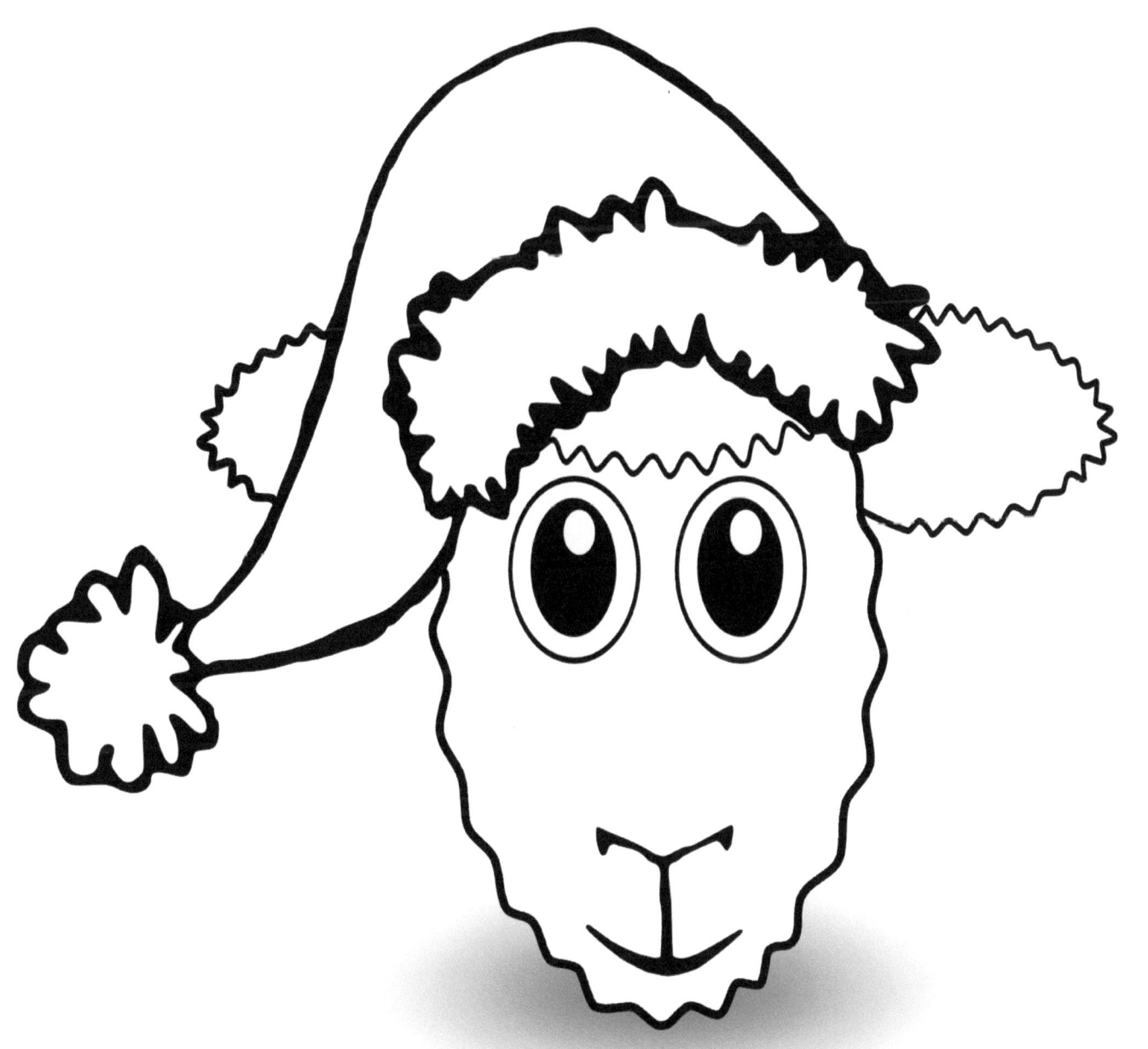

I Am A
S H E E P

I Am A

_ _ _ _ _ _

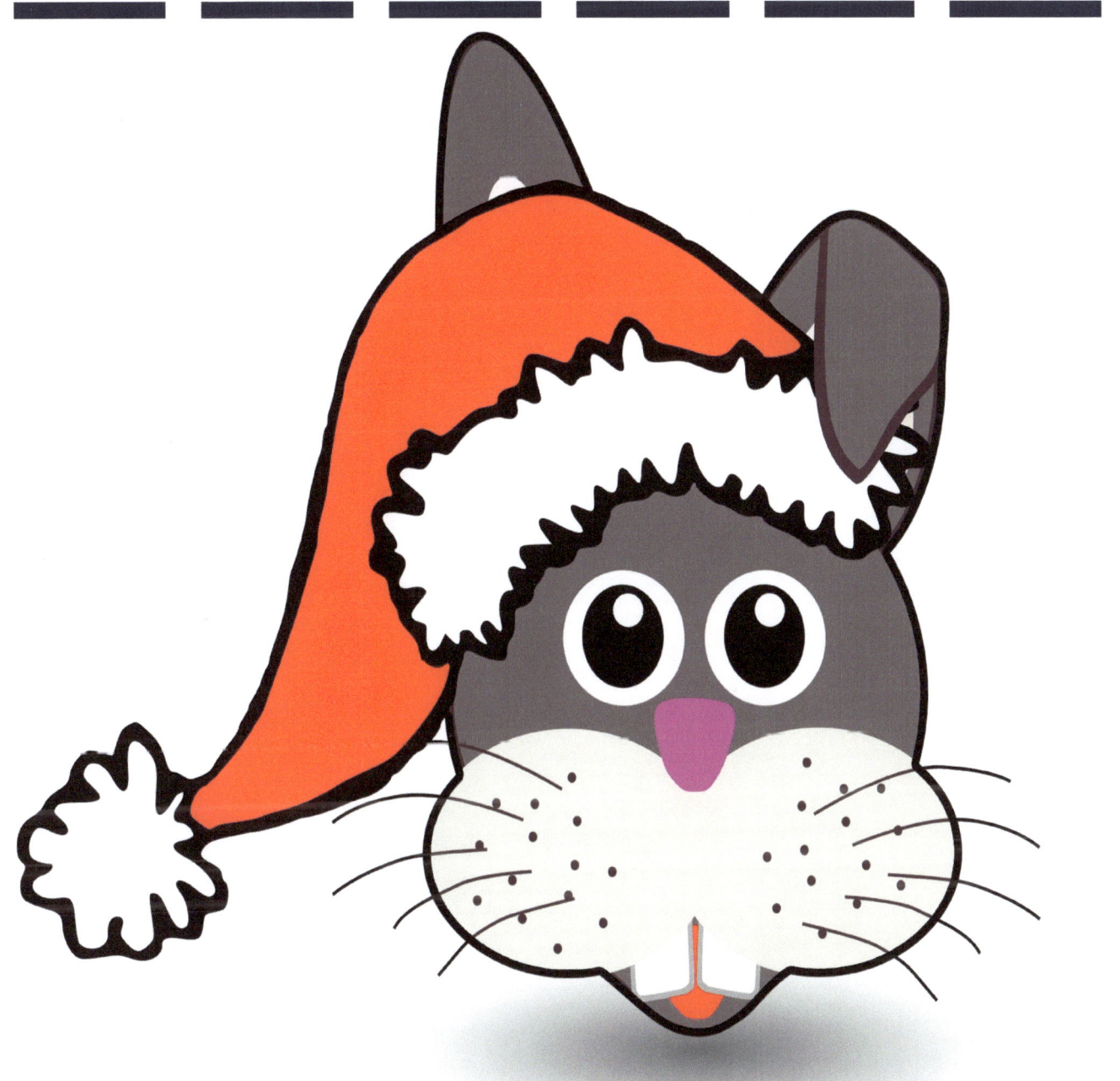

RABBIT

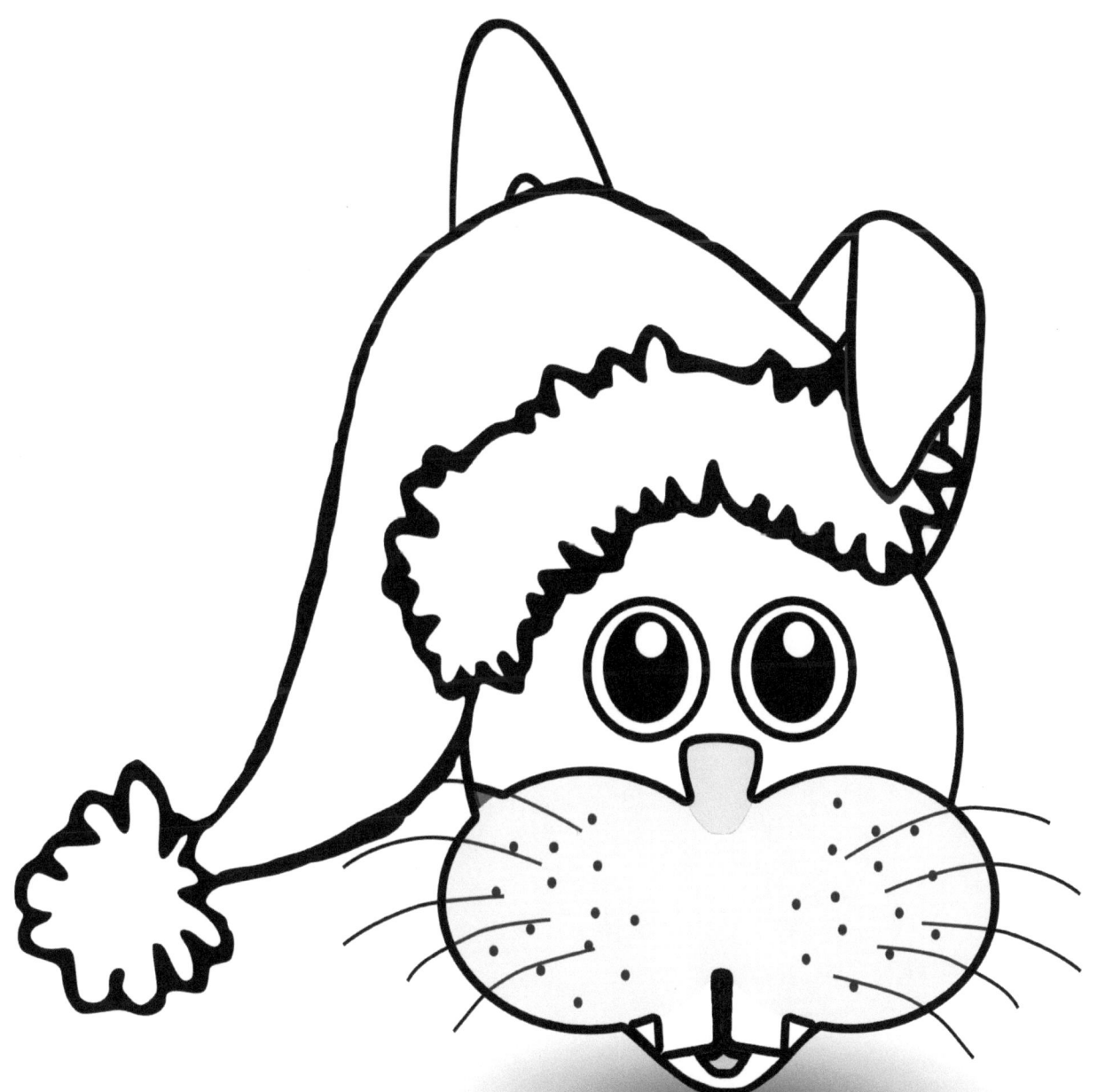

I Am A
RABBIT

I Am A

_ _ _ _ _ _ _

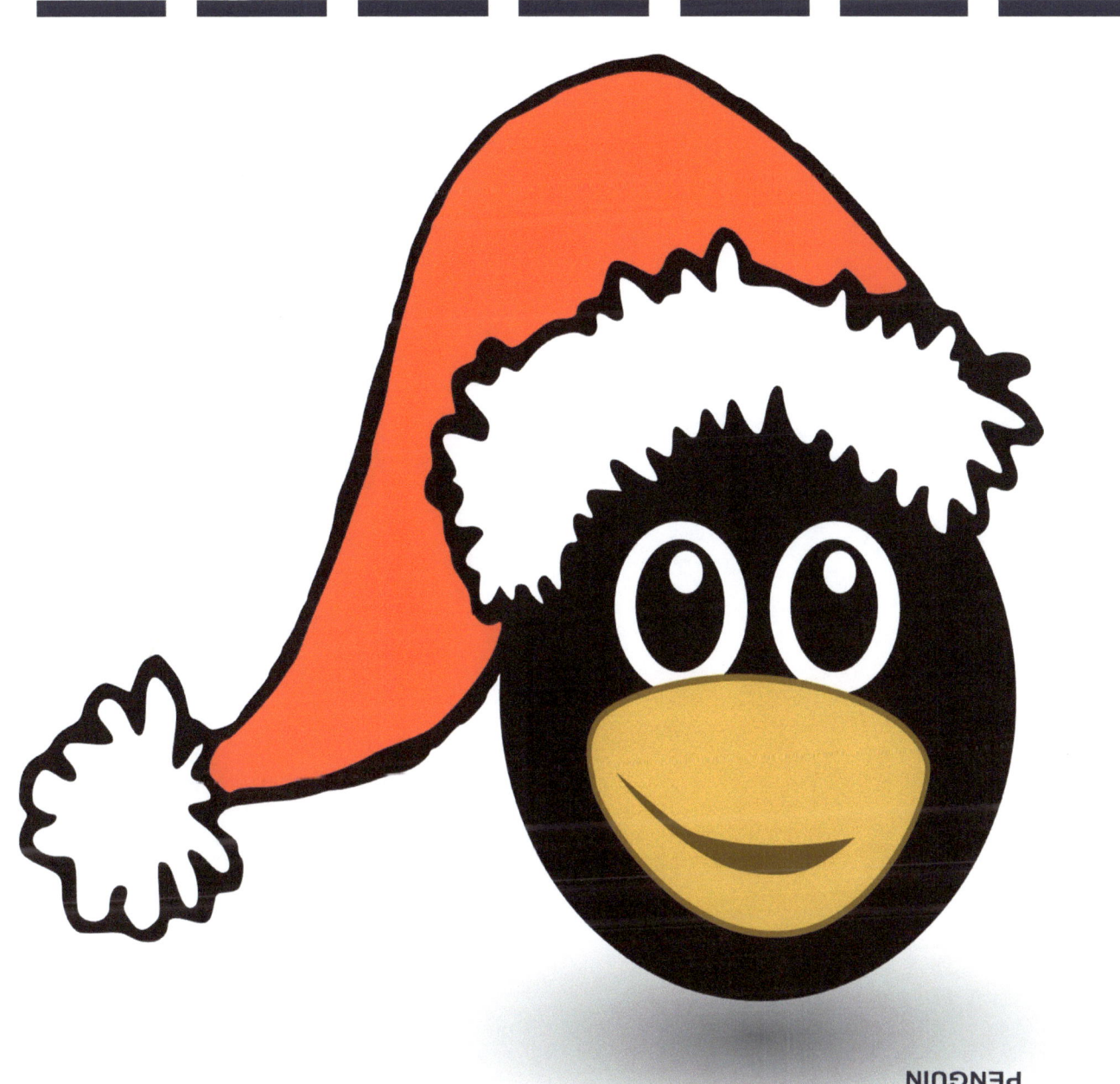

PENGUIN

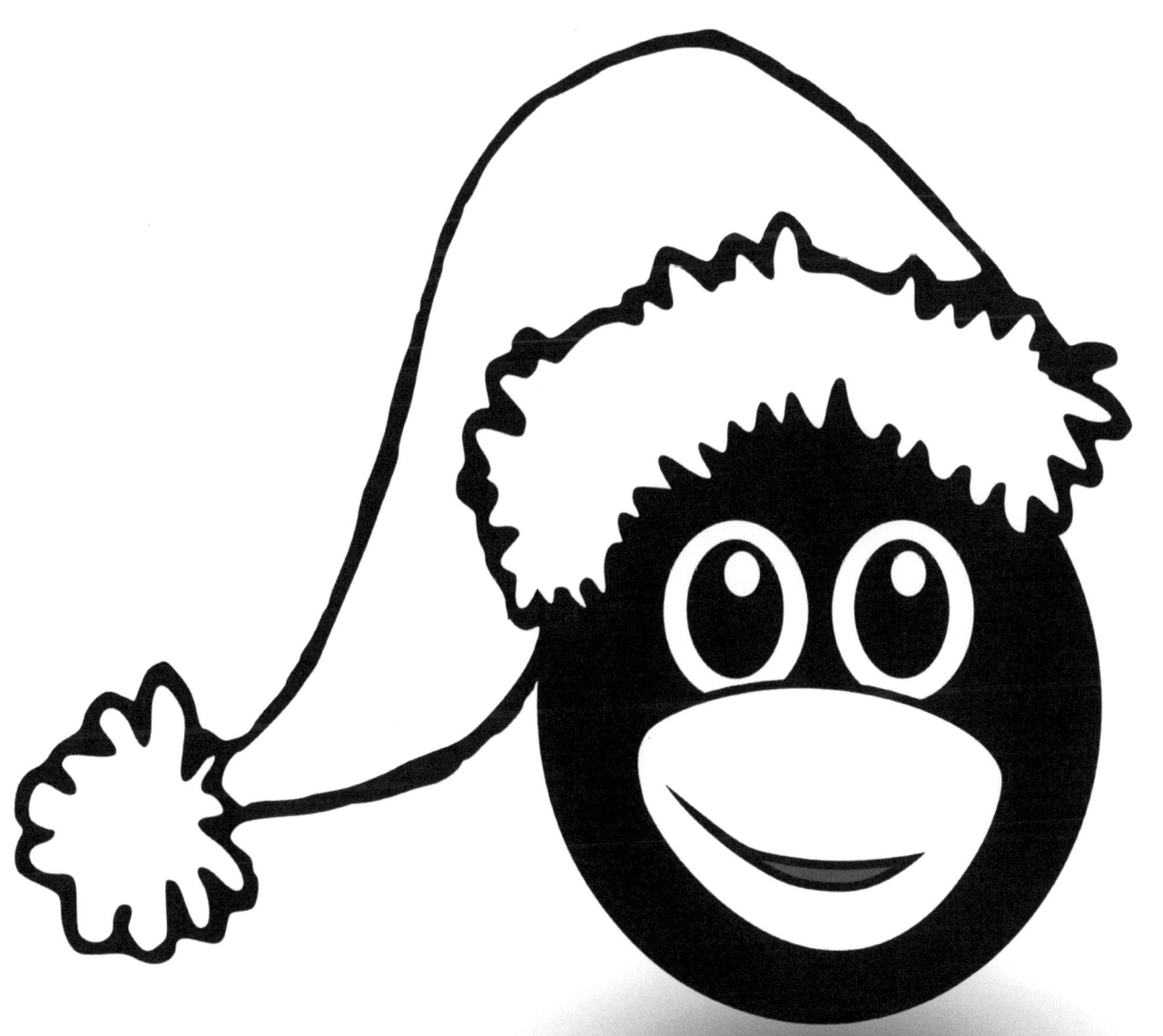

I Am A
PENGUIN

I Am A

_ _ _ _ _ _

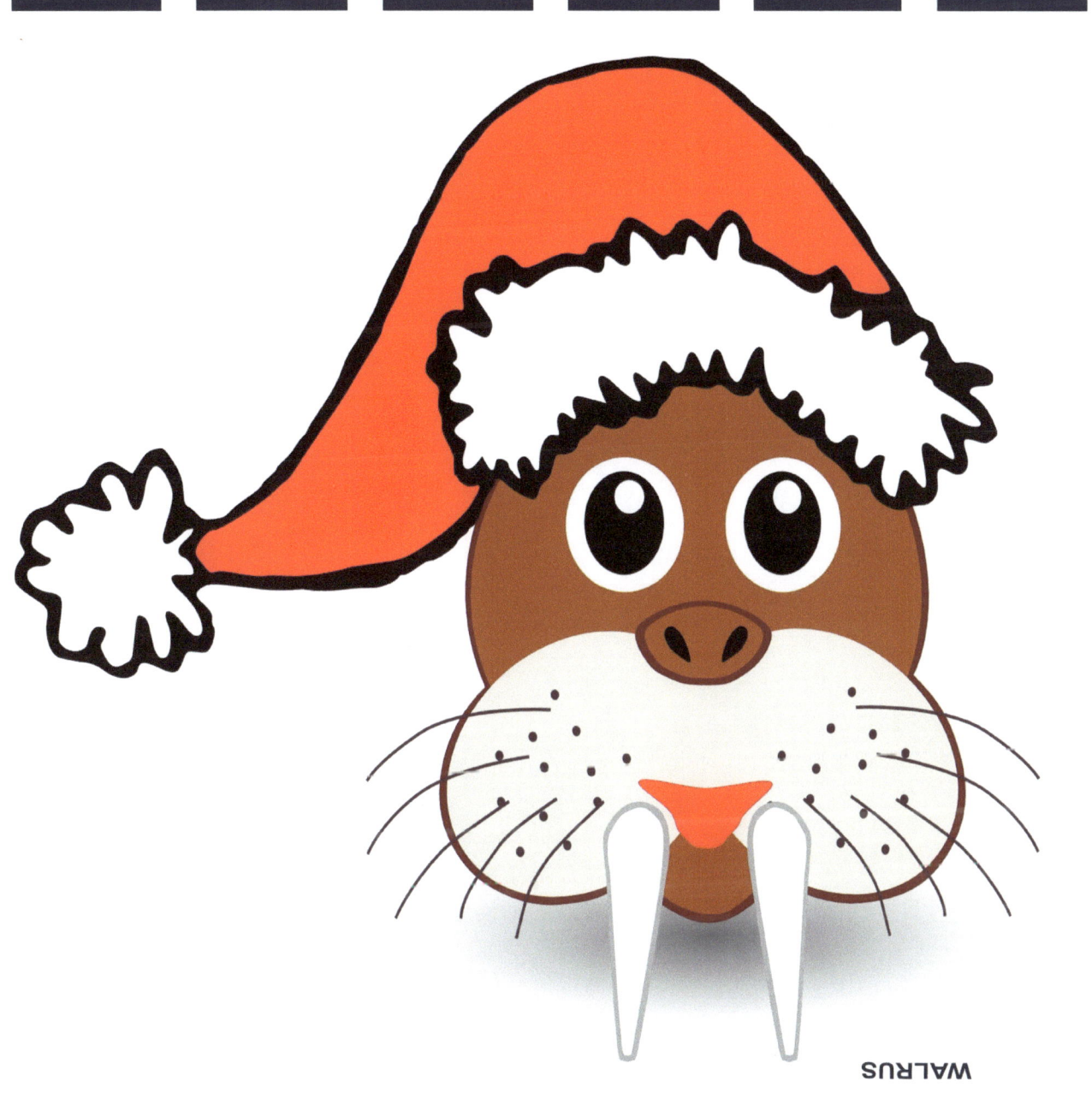

WALRUS

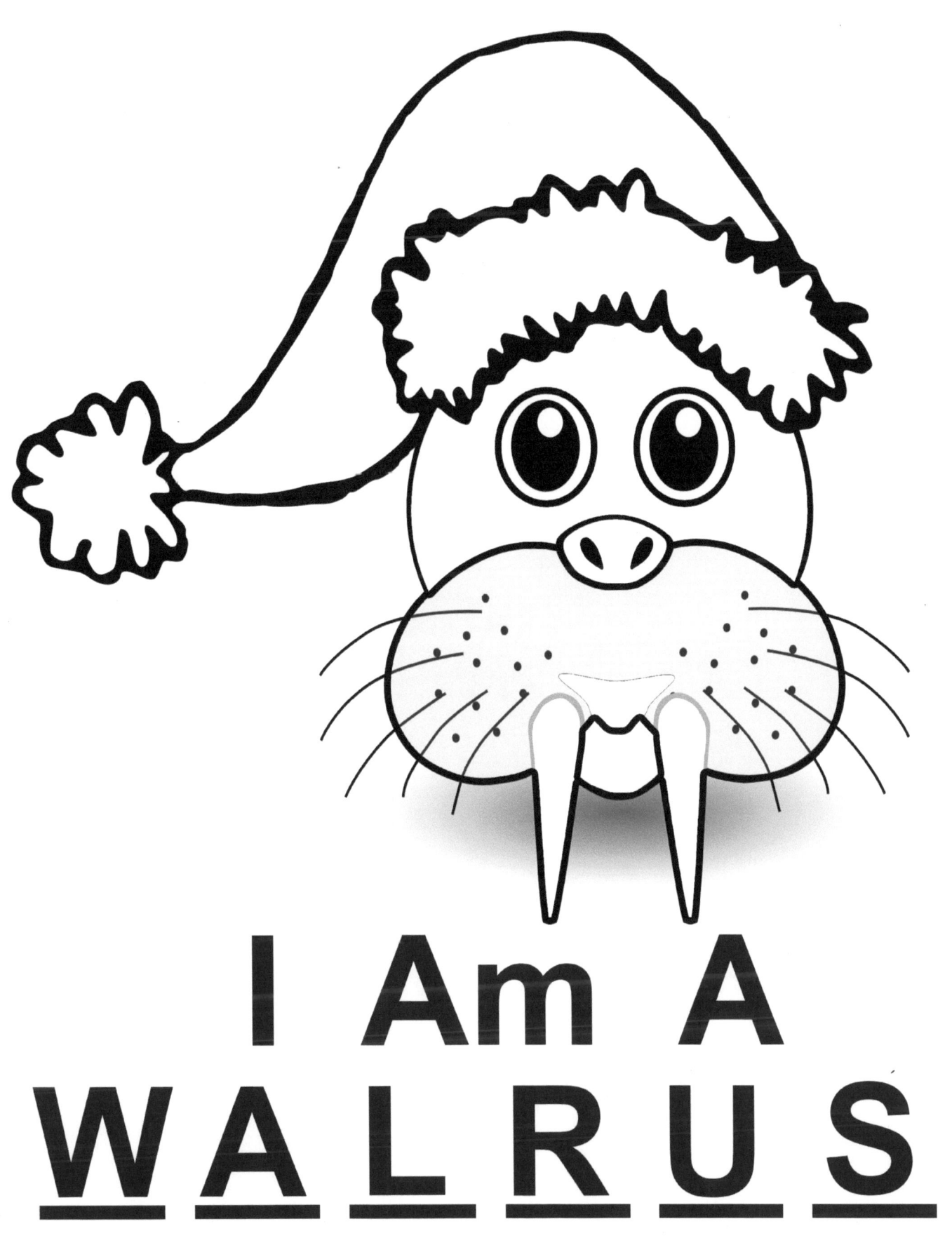

I Am A
WALRUS

I Am A

_ _ _ _ _ _ _ _ _

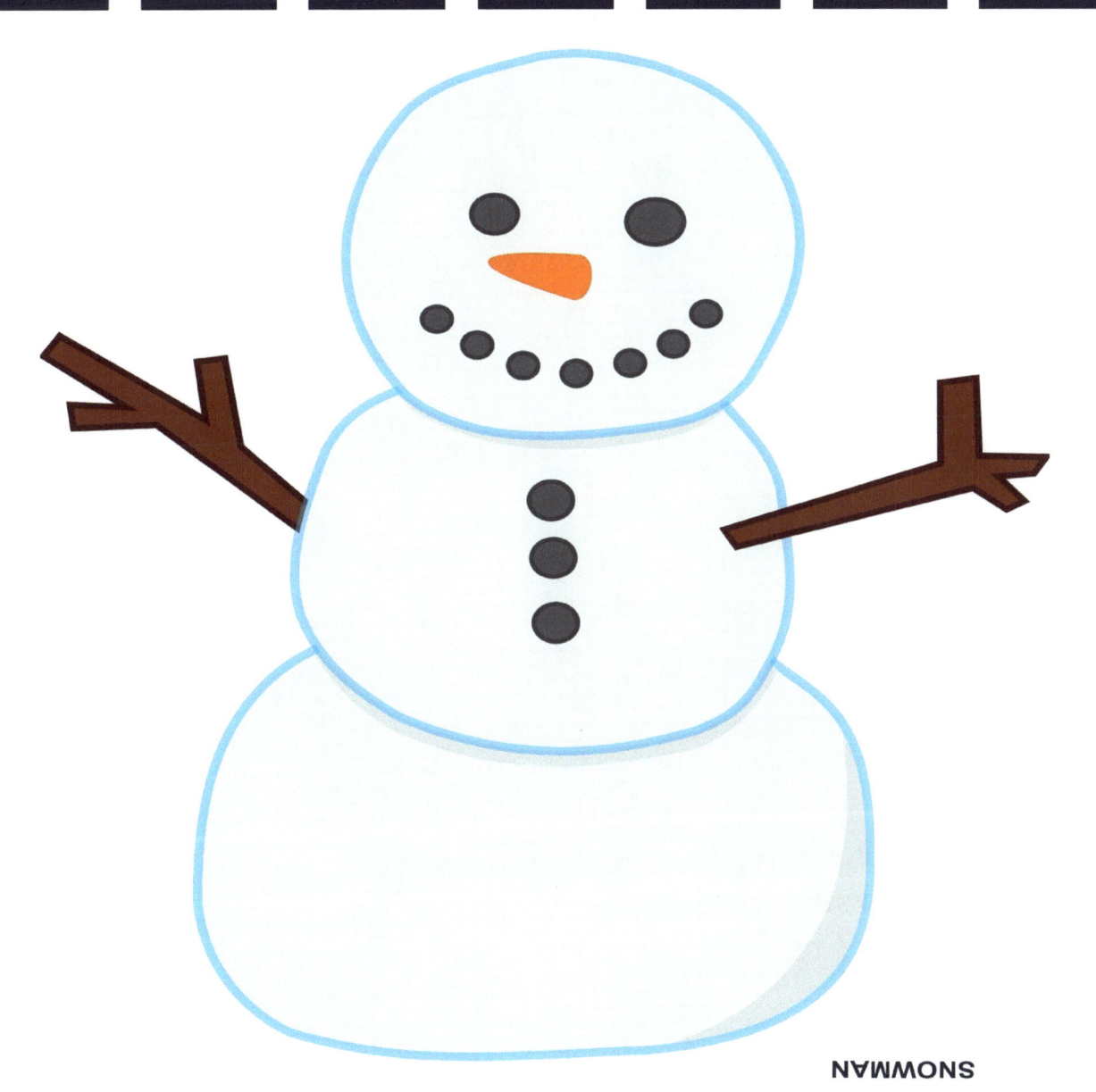

SNOWMAN

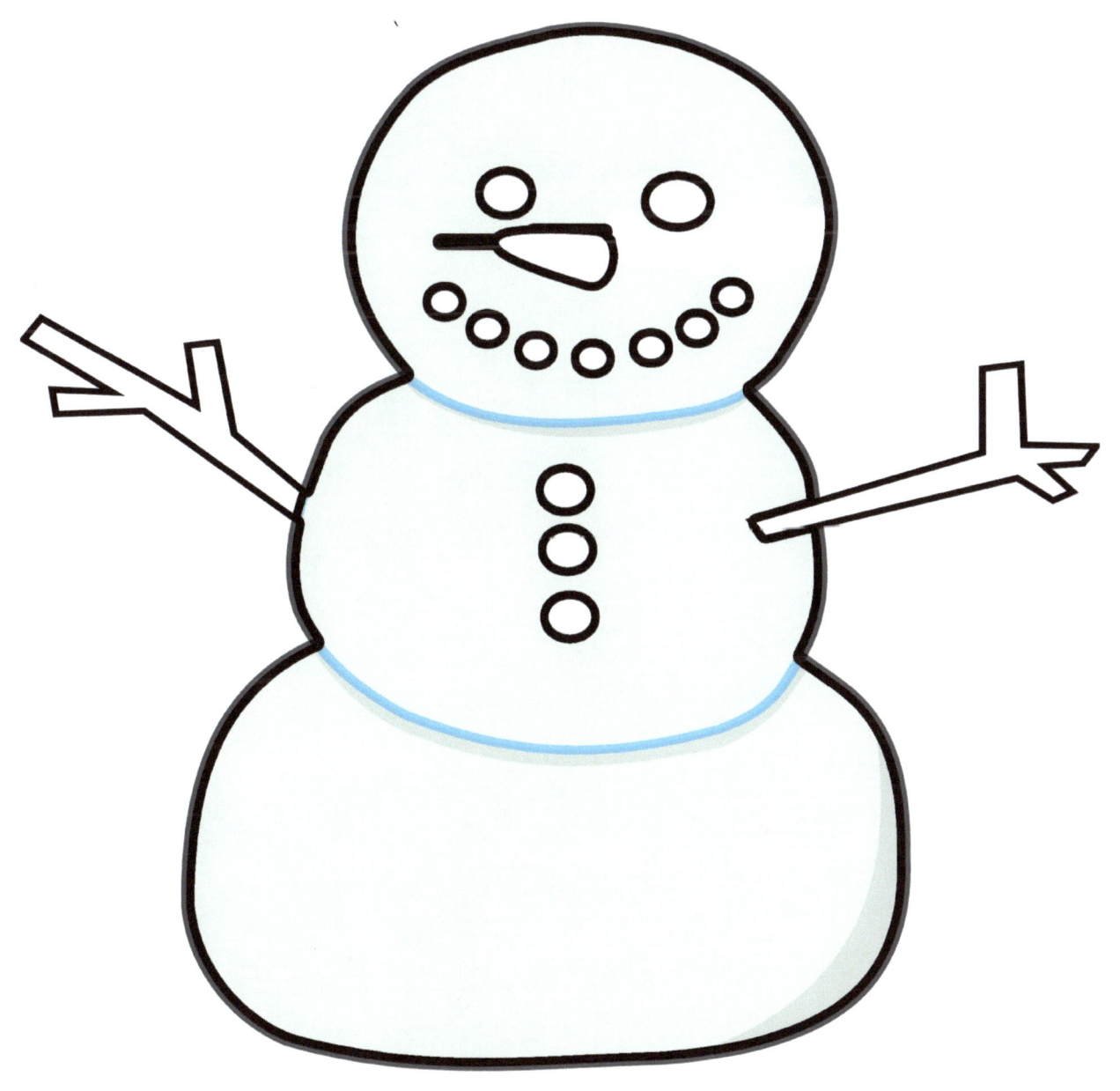

I Am A
SNOWMAN

We Are

_ _ _ _ _ _ _

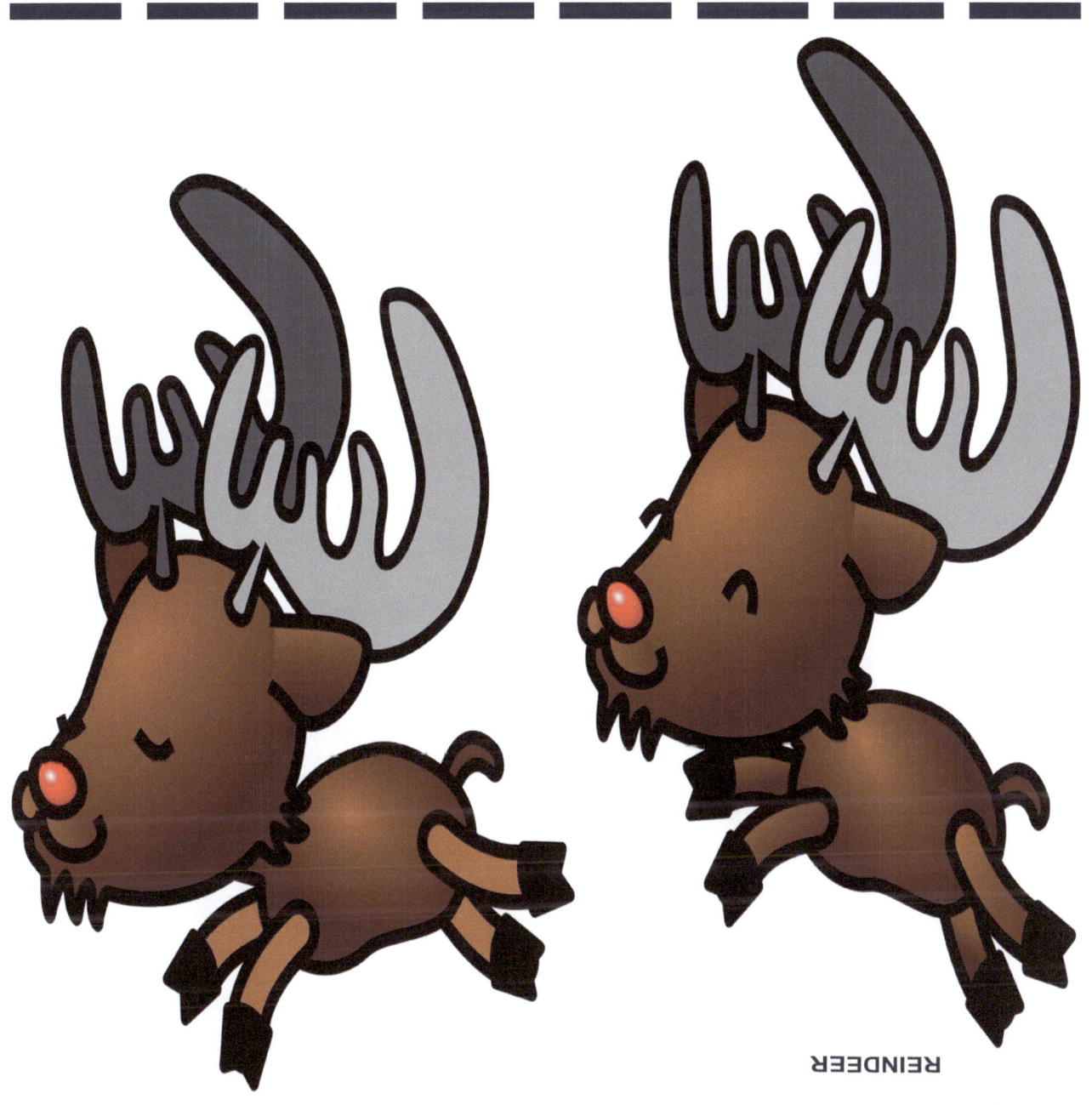

REINDEER

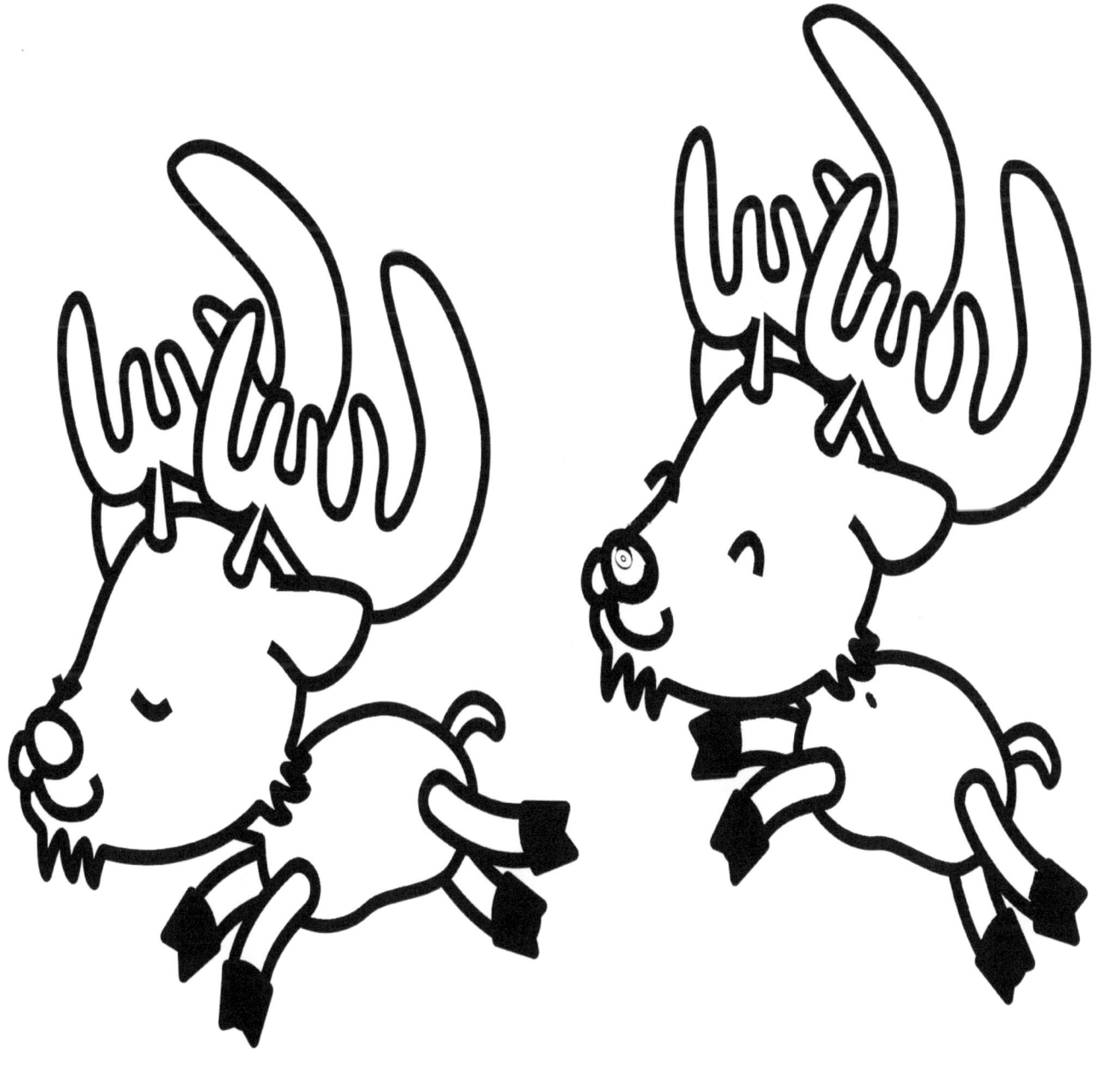

We Are
REINDEER

I Am

_ _ _ _ _ _

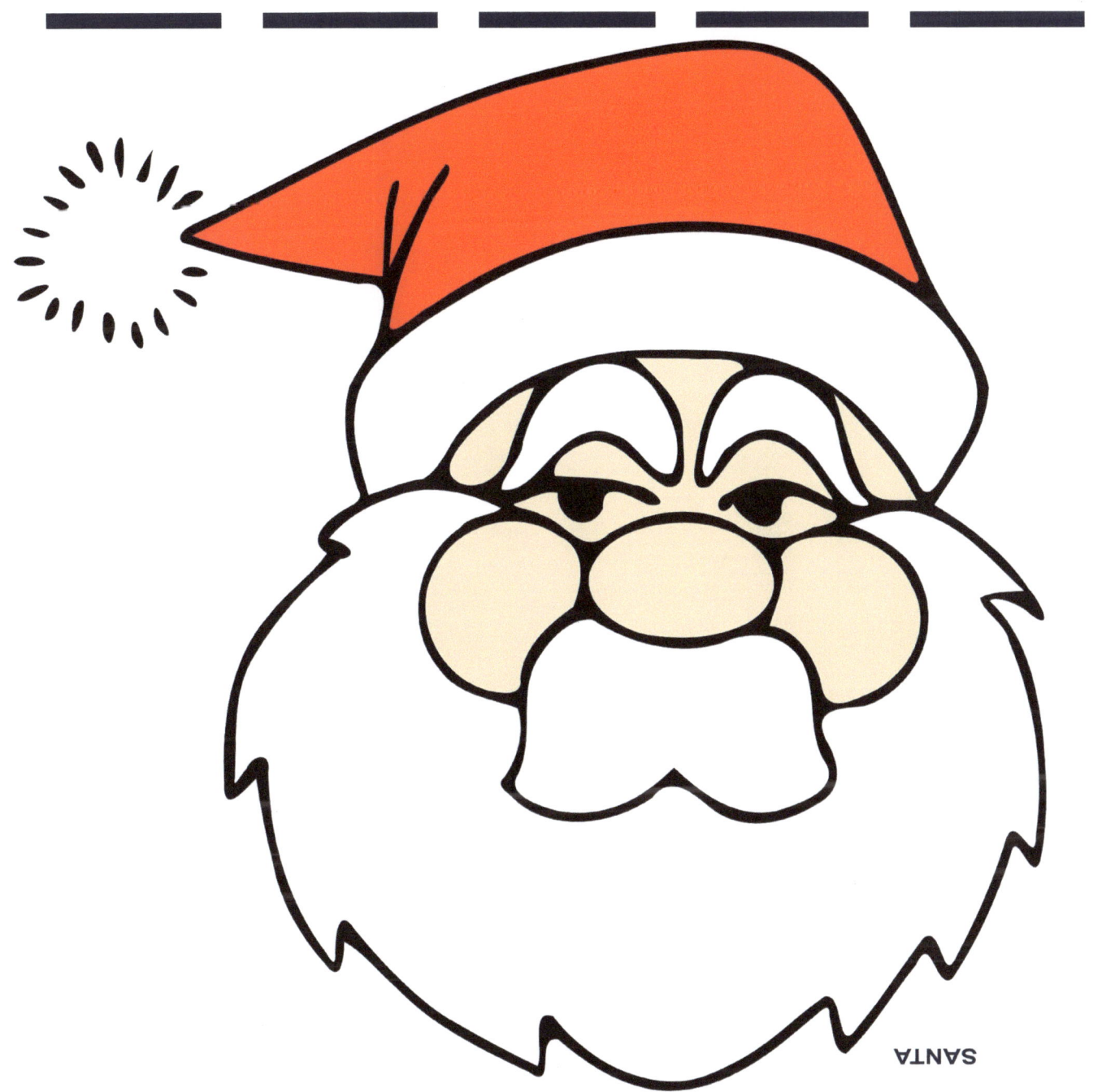

SANTA

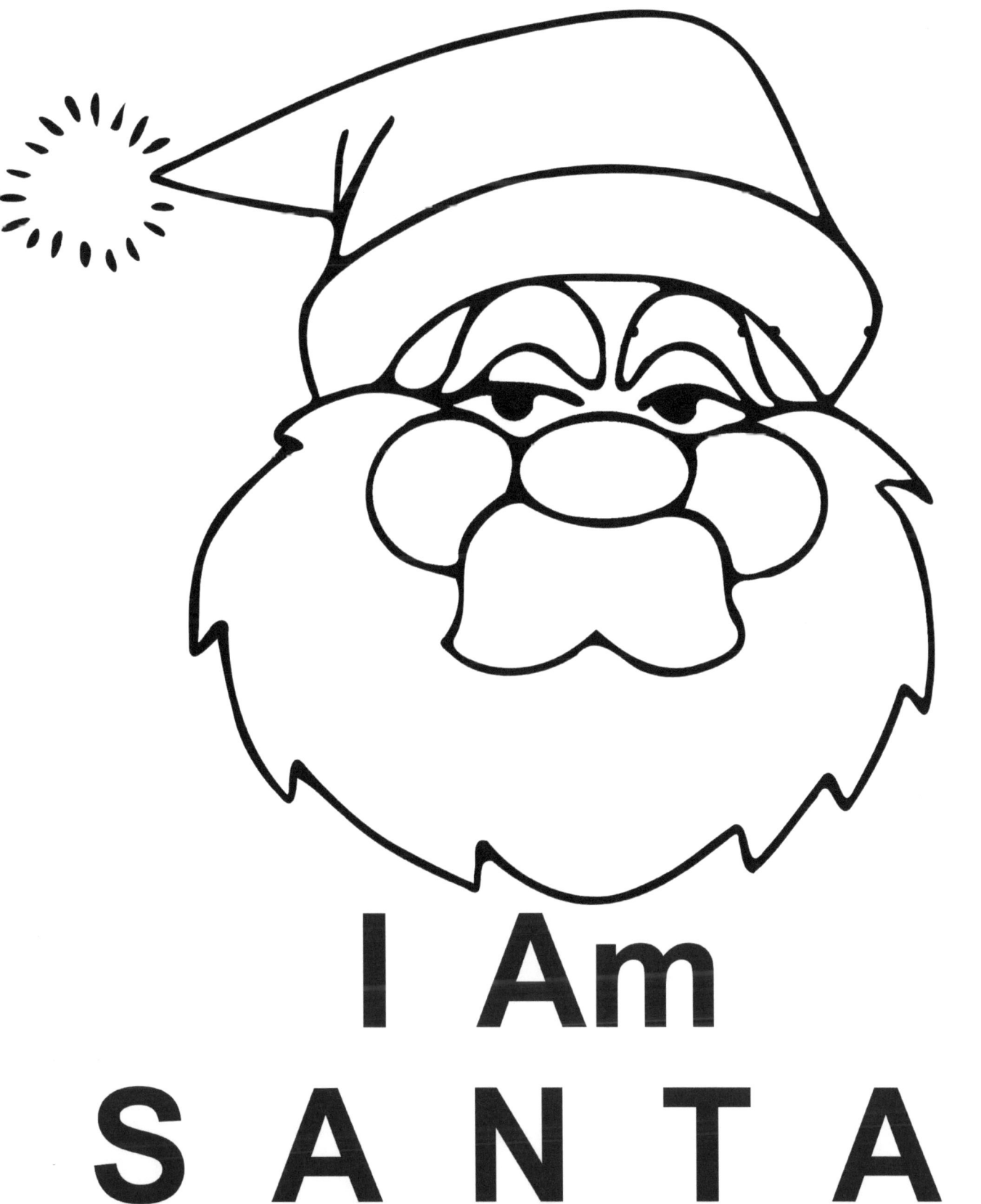

I Am
S A N T A

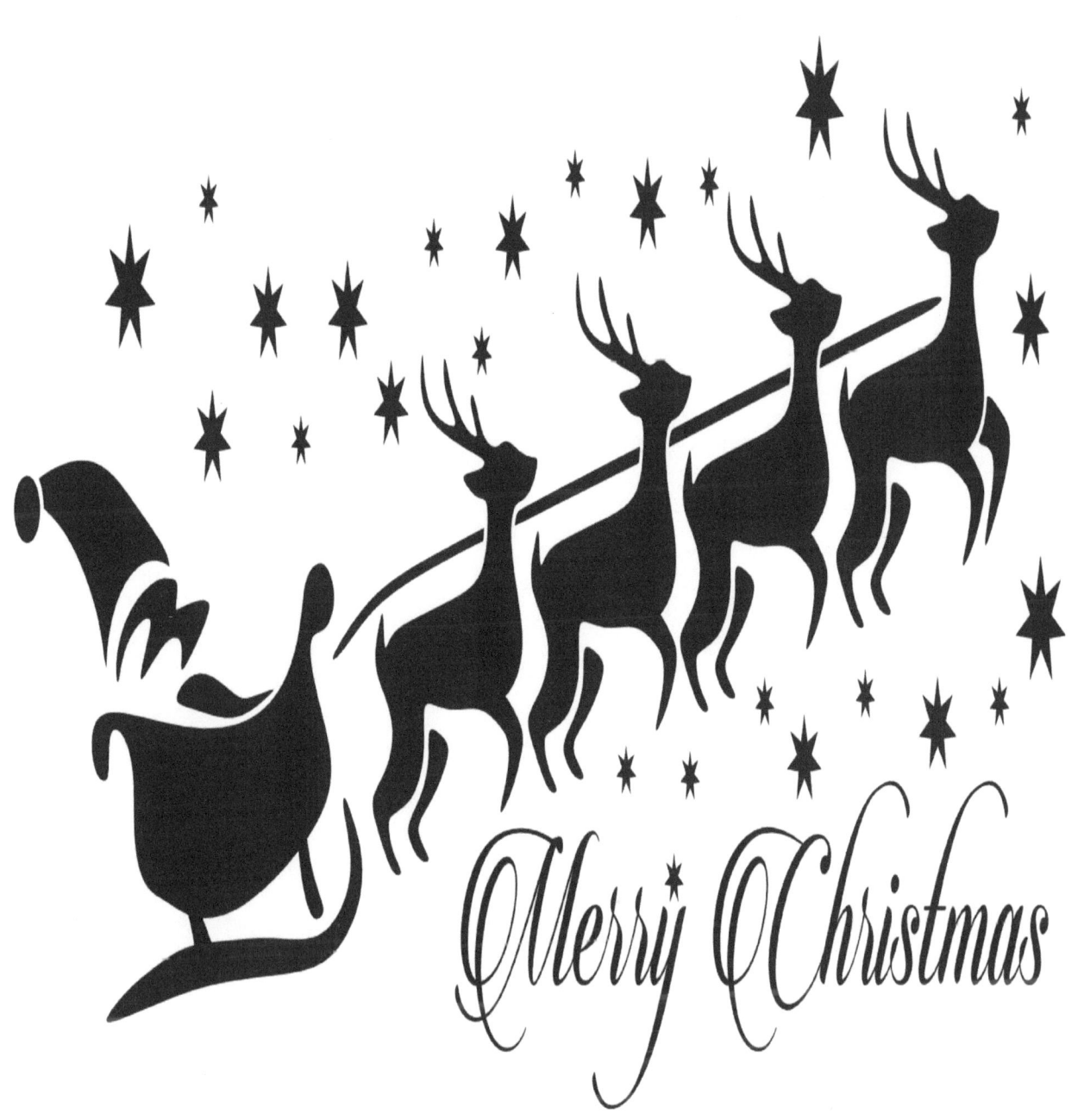

Merry Christmas